• Bartholomew •

Best Walks
IN
THE DALES

by Brian Spencer

Bartholomew
An Imprint of HarperCollins*Publishers*

CONTENTS

A Bartholomew Walk Guide
Published by Bartholomew
An Imprint of HarperCollins*Publishers*
77-85 Fulham Palace Road
London W6 8JB

First published 1996
Text © Brian Spencer 1996
Maps © Bartholomew 1996

The walks contained in this guide were first published in Bartholomew's Walk the Dales

Printed in Great Britain by
Scotprint Limited, Musselburgh

ISBN 0 7028 3520 X
96/1/16

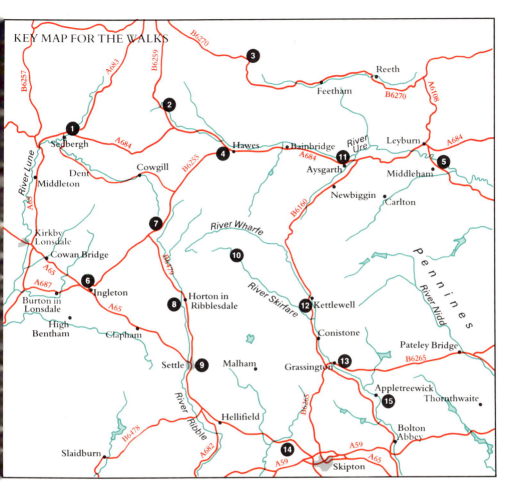

KEY MAP FOR THE WALKS

KEY TO SCALE AND MAP SYMBOLS

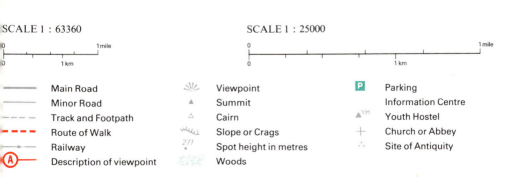

SCALE 1 : 63360

SCALE 1 : 25000

Main Road	
Minor Road	
Track and Footpath	
Route of Walk	
Railway	
(A) Description of viewpoint	

Viewpoint	
Summit	
Cairn	
Slope or Crags	
271 Spot height in metres	
Woods	

P Parking	
Information Centre	
▲YH Youth Hostel	
+ Church or Abbey	
Site of Antiquity	

3

INTRODUCTION

1 WALKING IN THE DALES

People have walked the Yorkshire Dales almost since the first man appeared on our shores. Prehistoric hunters followed regular routes along grassy ridges and across the broad cols connecting individual dales. Later, the Romans built their roads, some of which are now used by modern traffic. Others are still recognisable as stony tracks across the fells. One of them, across Cam Fell, appears in this guide. Drovers and pack-horsemen, the ancestors of today's long-distance lorry drivers, created green roads which can be traced for miles across the wild central moors. Corpse roads linking outlying hamlets to sanctified ground miles down the dale still exist but it is perhaps the local footpaths, connecting villages and farmsteads, which will give the most pleasure to a walker in the Dales.

Walking is a sport which can fulfil the needs of everyone. You can adapt it to suit your own preferences and it is one of the healthiest of activities. Your inclination might be to walk two or three miles along a gentle track instead of one of the more arduous long-distance routes but, whatever the walk, it will always improve your general well-being. Walking should be anything from an individual pastime to a family stroll, or maybe a group of friends enjoying the fresh air and open spaces of our countryside. There is no need for walking to be competitive and, to get the most from a walk, it shouldn't be regarded simply as a means of covering a given distance in the shortest possible time.

As with all other outdoor activities, walking is safe provided a few simple common-sense rules are followed:

a Make sure you are fit enough to complete the walk.

b Always try to let others know where you intend going.

c Be clothed adequately for the weather and always wear suitable footwear.

d Always allow plenty of time for the walk, especially if it is longer or harder than you have done before.

e Whatever the distance you plan to walk, always allow plenty of daylight hours unless you are absolutely certain of the route.

f If mist or bad weather come on unexpectedly, do not panic and try to remember the last certain feature which you have passed (road, farm, wood, etc). Then work out your route from that point on the map but be sure of your route before continuing.

g Do not dislodge stone on the high edges: there may be climbers or other walkers on the lower crags and slopes.

h Unfortunately, accidents can happen even on the easiest of walks. If this should be the case and you need the help of others, make sure that the injured person is safe in a place where no further injury is likely to occur. For example, the injured person should not be left on a steep hillside or in danger from falling rocks. If you cannot leave anyone with the injured person, and even if they are conscious, try to leave a written note explaining their injuries and whatever you have done in the way of first-aid treatment. Make sure you know exactly where you left them and then go to find assistance. If you meet a National Park Ranger, tell him or her what has happened. Otherwise, make your way to a telephone, dial 999 and ask for help. Unless the accident has happened within easy access of a road, it is the responsibility of the police to arrange evacuation. Always give accurate directions on how to find the casualty and, if possible, give an indication of the injuries involved.

i When walking in open country, learn to keep an eye on the immediate foreground while you admire the scenery or plan the route ahead. This may sound difficult, especially to a beginner but, once you can adapt to this method, your enjoyment will increase.

j It's best to walk at a steady pace, always on the flat of the feet as this is less tiring. Try not to walk directly up or downhill. A zig-zag route is a more comfortable way of negotiating a slope. Running directly downhill is a major cause of erosion on popular hillsides.

k When walking along a country road, walk on the right, facing the traffic. The exception to this rule is, when approaching a blind bend, the walker should cross over to the left and so have a clear view and also be seen in both directions.

l   Finally, always park your car where it will not cause inconvenience to other road users or prevent a farmer from gaining access to his fields. Make sure that you lock your car and hide any valuables before leaving or, preferably, carry them with you.

2   EQUIPMENT

Equipment, including clothing, footwear and rucksacks, is essentially a personal thing and depends on several factors, such as the type of activity planned, the time of year and weather likely to be encountered.

All too often, a novice walker will spend pounds on a fashionable jacket but will skimp when it comes to buying footwear or a comfortable rucksack. Blistered and tired feet quickly remove all enjoyment from even the most exciting walk and a poorly balanced rucksack will soon feel as though it is carrying half a hundredweight. Well designed equipment is not only more comfortable but, being better made, it is longer lasting.

Clothing should be adequate for the day. In summer, remember to protect your head and neck, which are particularly vulnerable in a strong sun. Wear light woollen socks and lightweight boots or strong shoes. A spare pullover and waterproofs carried in the rucksack should, however, always be there in case you need them.

Winter wear is a much more serious affair. Remember that once the body starts to lose heat, it becomes much less efficient. Jeans are particularly unsuitable for winter wear and can sometimes even be downright dangerous.

Waterproof clothing is an area where it pays to buy the best you can afford. Make sure that the jacket is loose-fitting, windproof, has a generous hood and comes down to at least knee level. Waterproof overtrousers will not only offer complete protection in the rain but they are also windproof. Do not be misled by flimsy nylon 'showerproof' affairs. Remember, too, that garments made from rubberised or plastic material are heavy to carry and wear and they trap body condensation. Your rucksack should have wide, padded carrying straps for comfort.

It is important to wear boots that fit well or shoes with a good moulded sole – blisters can ruin any walk! Woollen socks are much more comfortable than any other fibre. Your clothes should be comfortable and not likely to catch on twigs and bushes. In winter, it's best to take two lightweight jumpers, one at least with a crew neck. You will find this better than wearing one jumper made of heavy material. A woollen hat, which can be pulled well down, is essential in winter.

A piece of semi-rigid plastic foam carried in the rucksack makes a handy and yet almost weightless seat for open-air picnics.

An area map, as well as this guide, is useful for accurate navigation and it adds to the enjoyment of a walk. Finally, a small first aid kit is an invaluable help in coping with cuts and other small injuries.

3   PUBLIC RIGHTS OF WAY

Although most of the area covered by this guide comes within the authority of the Yorkshire Dales National Park, this does not mean that there is complete freedom of access to walk anywhere. Most of the land within the park is privately owned and what might appear to be an ideal spot for a picnic, or somewhere to exercise the dog, is often part of another person's livelihood.

In 1949, the *National Parks and Access to the Countryside Act* tidied up the law covering rights of way. Following public consultation, maps were drawn up by the Countryside Authorities of England and Wales to show all the rights of way. Copies of these maps are available for public inspection and are invaluable when trying to resolve doubts over little-used footpaths. Once on the map, the right of way is irrefutable.

Right of way means that anyone may walk freely on a defined footpath or ride a horse or pedal cycle along a public bridleway. No-one may interfere with this right and the walker is within his rights if he removes any obstruction along the route, provided that he has not set out purposely with the intention of removing that obstruction. All obstructions should be reported to the local Highways Authority.

Free access to footpaths and bridleways does mean that certain guidelines should be followed as a courtesy to those who live and work in the area. For example, you should only sit down to picnic where it does not interfere with other walkers or the landowner. All gates must be kept closed to prevent stock from straying and dogs must be kept under close control – usually this is interpreted as meaning that they should be kept on a leash. Motor vehicles must not be driven along a public footpath or bridleway without the landowner's consent.

A farmer can put a docile mature beef bull with a herd of cows or heifers, in a field crossed by a public footpath. Beef bulls such as Herefords (usually brown/red colour) are unlikely to be upset by passers-by but dairy bulls, like the black and white Friesian, can be dangerous by nature. It is, therefore, illegal for a farmer to let a dairy bull roam loose in a field open to public access.

Most public rights of way within the Yorkshire Dales National Park have been clearly defined and are marked as such on available maps. They are marked on the Ordnance Survey one inch (1:63 360) and metric (1:50 000) maps as red dots for footpaths and red dashes for bridleways. On the OS 1:25 000 scale, the dots and dashes are green (red dots and dashes on the 1:25 000 Outdoor Leisure Maps indicate concessionary footpaths and bridleways respectively). All of the walks in this guide cover routes which follow the public right of way, or concessionary footpaths.

4   THE COUNTRY CODE

The Country Code has been designed not as a set of hard and fast rules, although they do have the backing of the law, but as a statement of common sense. The code is a gentle reminder of how to behave in the countryside. Walkers should walk with the intention of leaving the place exactly as it was before they arrived. There is a saying that a good walker 'leaves only footprints and takes only photographs', which really sums up the code perfectly.

Never walk more than two abreast on a footpath as you will erode more ground by causing an unnatural widening of paths. Also try to avoid the spread of trodden ground around a boggy area. Mud soon cleans off boots but plant life is slow to grow back once it has been worn away.

Have respect for everything in the countryside, be it those beautiful flowers found along the way or a farmer's gate which is difficult to close.

Stone walls were built at a time when labour costs were a fraction of those today and the special skills required to build or repair them have almost disappeared. Never climb over or onto stone walls; always use stiles and gates.

Dogs which chase sheep can cause them to lose their lambs and a farmer is within his rights if he shoots a dog which he believes is worrying his stock.

The moors and woodlands are often tinder dry in summer, so take care not to start a fire. A fire caused by something as simple as a discarded cigarette can burn for weeks, once it gets deep down into the underlying peat.

When walking across fields or enclosed land, make sure that you read the map carefully and avoid trespassing. As a rule, the line of a footpath or right of way, even when it is not clearly defined on the ground, can usually be followed by lining up stiles or gates.

5   MAP READING

Some people find map reading so easy that they can open a map and immediately relate it to the area of countryside in which they are standing. To others, a map is as unintelligible as ancient Greek! A map is an accurate but flat picture of the three-dimensional features of the countryside. Features such as roads, streams, woodland and buildings are relatively easy to identify, either from their shape or position. Heights, on the other hand, can be difficult to interpret from the single dimension of a map. The one inch (1:63 360) maps indicate every 50 foot contour line, while the metricated 1:25 000 and 1:50 000 maps give the contours at 10 metre intervals. Summits and spot heights are also shown.

The best way to estimate the angle of a slope, as shown on any map, is to remember that if the contour lines come close together then the slope is steep – the closer the steeper.

Learn the symbols for features shown on the map and, when starting out on a walk, line up the map with one or more feature, which is recognisable both from the map and on the ground. In this way, the map will be correctly positioned relative to the terrain. It should only be necessary to look from the map towards the footpath or objective of your walk and then make for it! This process is also useful for determining your position at any time during the walk.

Let's take the skill of map reading one stage further. Sometimes there are no easily recognisable features nearby. There may be the odd clump of trees and a building or two but none of them can be related exactly to the map. This is a frequent occurrence but there is a simple answer to the problem and this is where the use of a compass comes in. Simply place the map on the ground, or other flat surface, with the compass held gently above the map. Turn the map until the edge is parallel to the line of the compass needle, which should point to the top of the map. Lay the compass on the map and adjust the position of both, making sure that the compass needle still points to the top of the map and is parallel to the edge. By this method, the map is orientated in a north-south alignment. To find your position on the map, look out for prominent features and draw imaginary lines from them down on to the map. Your position is where these lines cross. This method of map reading takes a little practice before you can become proficient but it is worth the effort.

It is all too easy for members of a walking group to leave map reading to the skilled member or members of the party. No one is perfect and even the best map reader can make mistakes. Other members of the group should take the trouble to follow the route on the map, so that any errors are spotted before they cause problems.

Once you become proficient at map reading, you will learn to estimate the length of time required for a walk. Generally, you should estimate an extra five minutes for every 100 feet (30.5m) you walk uphill.

6 THE YORKSHIRE DALES NATIONAL PARK

In many other countries, National Parks are wilderness areas, where few people live unless they are connected with running the park. Countries such as the United States of America have even gone to the length of moving residents off land designated as a National Park. In England and Wales, National Parks are areas of outstanding beauty where people still live and work. One of the major functions of a National Park is to preserve the landscape and the livelihoods of the people living within its boundaries. This is achieved by careful planning control. The *National Parks and Access to the Countryside Act* of 1949 led to the formation of the nine National Parks in England and Wales.

The word National in the title sometimes leads to misunderstanding. National Parks are not nationalised or in any way owned by the government.

The Yorkshire Dales National Park was formed in 1953 and covers an area of approximately 680 square miles (1760 sq.km). It is controlled by a committee nominated by the North Yorkshire County Council and representatives of three district councils, whose areas encroach into the park: Craven, Richmondshire and South Lakeland. This committee is augmented by a further eight members (one-third of the total) appointed by the Secretary of State for the Environment to represent the wider national interests in this national asset.

Large areas of grouse moorland, mainly in the south of the park are held by the Chatsworth Estates Trust for the Duke of Devonshire. Rights of Way cross several of the moors but, most importantly, the estate allows free access to Barden and Simonseat Moors above Bolton Abbey on either side of Wharfedale. This means that walkers have the right to roam freely over the moors on all but publicised days during the shooting season or during periods of high fire risk. This concession is one which must be respected by all users.

One of the statutory functions of a Park Authority is the appointment of full-time and voluntary Park Rangers. These are people with particular knowledge of some aspects of the local environment who are available to give help and advice to visitors.

There are six full-time Information Centres based at Aysgarth, Clapham, Grassington, Hawes, Malham and Sedbergh, together with Tourist Information Centres at Bentham, Brough, Harrogate, Ilkley, Ingleton, Kirkby Lonsdale, Kirkby Stephen, Knaresborough, Leyburn, Pateley Bridge, Richmond, Ripon and Settle on the outskirts of the park. A number of village shops throughout the Dales can now give local information on holiday accommodation, sell walking guides and offer other information to back up the full-time Information Centres. These shops are at Askrigg, Bolton Abbey, Buckden, Dent, Gunnerside, Hebden, Horsehouse, Horton, Kettlewell, Langcliffe, Litton, Muker, Reeth and Stump Cross.

There is an Outdoor Study and Recreation Centre at Whernside Manor in Dentadale, where residential and day courses are offered by the National Park Authority in subjects ranging from fell walking to caving and general field studies. Cycle tours are organised and special rambling weekends are arranged throughout the year.

7 WHAT ARE THE YORKSHIRE DALES?

The Central Pennines are cut by a series of valleys which have become known as the

Yorkshire Dales. Radiating from a watershed on the mass of high ground north and east of Ribblehead, five rivers, the Swale , Ure, Nidd, Wharfe and Aire, eventually flow east into the North Sea by way of the Ouse and Humber. Three others, the Ribble, Lune and Eden, all enter the Irish Sea, to the west, as independent rivers. All have their birth on the gritstone cap of the central moors but, with the exception of the Nidd and Lune, they all flow for at least their middle sections through countryside based upon limestone. As a result, the rivers have carved deep clefts through the soluble limestone rock to reach harder, watertight shales and slates.

Every dale has its own character. In the north, Swaledale is the wildest, a deep-cut gorge below rolling heather moors, joined by its even wilder tributary, Arkengarthdale, at Reeth where the dale begins to take on a gentler aspect. Villages of stone-built cottages line its northern banks. Place names can be traced to the early Viking settlers.

The next east-flowing dale is Wensleydale, the only one which does not take its name from its river, in this case the Ure. Wensleydale was once filled by a glacial lake and its flatter valley bottom and wider aspect is the result. Lush meadowlands feed the dairy cattle which produce milk for the famous Wensleydale cheese. The dale is renowned for its waterfalls but less appreciated features are in its four side dales, all roughly parallel to each other, which flow from the south-west. These often secluded valleys will reward anyone who wants to explore their secrets.

Next is Nidderdale, a little-known dale to the east of Wharfedale, where the strangely-worn shapes of Brimham Rocks cut into the skyline. In fact, Nidderdale is not part of the Yorkshire Dales National Park.

Wharfedale and Airdale, with their ease of access from the West Riding, are probably the best known dales. Wharfedale, wooded in its lower reaches, is lined with dramatic limestone formations and attractive villages, a feature echoed by its tributary, Littondale, for all except its sombre headwaters. Airedale's Malham Cove, an amphitheatre of solid limestone, is an outstanding feature of the Dales. A tributary of the Aire flows from its base – the main river still flows underground at this point. The ravine of Gordale Scar, a roofless cave, is close by.

Of the western dales, Ribblesdale is essentially a limestone dale separating the three highest summits of the Dales, Whernside, Ingleborough and Penyghent. Like the other northern rivers which flow into the Irish Sea, its waters are clean enough to welcome sea trout and salmon. It is the Lune's tributaries, Dentdale and Garsdale which are completely within the boundaries of the National Park, the main dale mostly skirting the north-west edge. Of the Eden, only its highest tributary, Hell Gill with its fantastic ravine, is within the park, its headwaters forming the county boundary of Cumbria and North Yorkshire, a boundary followed by the National Park.

The earliest settlers in the Dales were the hunters who lived in caves such as Victoria Cave above Settle, where the remains of reindeer and bones of grizzly bears have been found, animals which lived on the tundra-like conditions following the Ice Age. As man became more settled he built enigmatic cairns and stone circles, the use of which we can only surmise. With the Roman invasion, roads began to appear across the fells and forts were built to control lead mining areas. Lead increased in value with the expansion of building from Roman times, through the height of monastic power right up to the 19th century when cheaper imports killed off the local industry with devastating effect. Remains of the old lead mines and their smelt houses can still be found on the moors above Swaledale and Wensleydale in the north and near Grassington in the south.

Monasteries developed in the Middle Ages to cement an enforced peace made after the Norman Conquest. With their power, which only ended with the Dissolution in the 16th century, they exploited with riches of the lead mines and encouraged the development of vast flocks of sheep which roamed unhindered for miles across the fells, setting the scene for farming patterns which have changed only in recent years. The next development to take place was the movement of animals and goods across the moors; animals were driven south from Scotland and the Dales by a tough breed of men known as drovers. These men slowly moved their charges to the rapidly growing industrial areas further south, by routes which can still be traced to this day. Many of the old drove roads and pack-horse routes are still clearly defined as 'green roads', which snake for miles across the high fells and limestone plateaux of the Dales.

Today's Dalesman retains much of the character of his forebears, generally taciturn, but once you have broken through his natural reserve he becomes a friend and informant of the background to the fascinating life and environment of the Dales. The Dales themselves have a character all of their own, unique within the British Isles; like their people, the Dales need to be understood to be appreciated.

8   GEOLOGY

Almost 300 million years ago, the rocks which today are the lowest part of the Yorkshire Dales, existed as the muddy floor of a shallow tropical sea. Those muds became slates, the bedrock of many of the Dales' rivers. Gradually the sea filled with the teeming life of tiny crustaceans living amongst long-stemmed waterlily-like plants. As these plants and animals died, their bodies and shells sank slowly to the bottom of the sea, consolidating to form the collosal limestone cover which features so predominately throughout the Dales. Much later, a huge river delta began to fill this sea, its outer deposits spreading to form shales, and on top of them came the harder gritstones, now the top-most rocks of the highest peaks.

As all this building up and smothering was taking place, land mass moved and gradually the land which was once in the tropics moved north towards its present position. During all this activity, faults occurred in the surface of the land. Rocks moved up and down; Malham Cove is a good surface example of a fault line.

While the land was beginning to settle into its present shape, subterranean activity forced hot mineral solutions of ores into narrow cracks in the upper rocks. These mineral solutions were mostly lead but there were traces of silver and even gold. Chemical reactions formed calcium fluoride, which was a nuisance to later miners but is a useful raw material today. To the north, vast upsurges of basalt created the columns of the Whin Sill.

Around 10,000 years BC, the land, though covered by ice, was beginning to take on the outline of the Dales as we know them. As the ice melted, moraine dams created lakes in areas such as Upper Wensleydale. Mud made from ground down rocks of the high tops began to form the basis of new strata and the process of wearing down and building up began again. In geological time 10,000 years is like a few minutes to us and, once the moraine dams were breached, those muds and clays began to form the basis of today's rich pastures of the Central Dales. The process is continuing.

9   WILDLIFE IN THE DALES

Wildlife habitats follow closely-defined zonal limits; on the hightops of Ingleborough and Penyghent, habitats are restricted to mosses and a little grass with alpine flowers, such as purple saxifrage (*Sax oppositifolia*), living in tiny crevices and ledges on the limestone crags. Mountains with broader summits, such as Whernside, are able to support coarse grasses, with heather and bilberry dominating the grouse moors further south. Meadow pipits and ring ouzels frequent the higher slopes and the dipper follows streams high on the fell. Birds of prey such as kestrels, merlins and buzzards, as well as the ubiquitous crow, can be found on most of the quieter fells. Mountain hares are often seen gambolling on the open hillsides. Even though standing water is rare on the normally dry cols and ridges, sea-birds, such as black-headed gulls, nest far from their 'official' home. For centuries, the land below the 1700 foot (520m) contour, has been improved for sheep grazing and true native grasses and rushes will only be found in areas of poor husbandry and under-grazing. Mountain pansy (*viola lutea*), rock rose (*helianthemum chamaecistus*) and thyme (*thymus serpyllum*), grow on sparse limestone soils. Limestone pavements are cracked and fissured by 'grikes' where the shade-loving plants such as dog's mercury (*mercuriatis perennis*) and hart's tongue fern (*phyllitis scolopendi*) are the remains of ground cover of native ash woods which covered the Dales before the last Ice Age.

Where the river-banks are uncultivated, natural woodland takes advantage of the rich damp soil and woodland flowers grow in profusion. Many of the rivers have excellent fish stocks but the best by far are the Lune and Ribble and their tributaries. Both main rivers manage to enter the Irish Sea relatively unpolluted and, as a result, are visited by migrant trout and spawning salmon.

10 LONG DISTANCE WALKS

Pennine Way: the first long-distance walking route in Britain. Starts from Edale in Derbyshire and follows a high-level route to Kirk Yetholm in the Scottish Borders. Enters the Yorkshire Dales at Gargrave and takes a more or less northerly course to Tan Hill and beyond.

Dales Way: from Ilkley, the way follows Wharfedale, then by way of Dentdale to Bowness-on-Windermere in the Lake District.

Coast to Coast: across the North of England from St. Bees Head on the Cumbrian Coast to Ravenscar on the North Yorkshire coast.

Ribble Valley Way: follows the river Ribble from its source to the sea near Preston in Lancashire.

11 SHOW CAVES OPEN TO THE PUBLIC

Ingleborough Cave: at the head of Clapdale. It can only be approached by footpath from Clapham or on the return from walks on Ingleborough.

Stump Cross Caverns: on the B6265 between Pateley Bridge and Grassington. A moorland footpath links the cave with Grimwith Reservoir.

White Scar Cave: at the side of the B6255 north-east of Ingleton. Could be visited as an extension to the Ingleton's Waterfalls walk.

12 USEFUL ADDRESSES

Yorkshire Dales National Park
Hebden Road
Grassington
Skipton
North Yorks BD23 5LB
Tel: (01756) 752748

Yorkshire Wildlife Trust Ltd
10 Toft Green, York
North Yorks YO1 1JT
Tel: (01904) 659570

National Park Information Centres:
Aysgarth Falls tel: (01969) 663424; Clapham tel: (015242) 51419; Grassington tel: (01756) 752774; Hawes tel: (01969) 667450; Malham tel: (01729) 830363; Sedbergh tel: (015396) 20125.

Dales-Rail (Settle-Carlisle line and bus links): c/o Yorkshire Dales National Park (*see* address and telephone number above).

Yorkshire Dales Railway: (short length of track with a good collection of steam locomotives run at weekends and bank holidays in summer) Embsay, Nr Skipton tel: (01756) 10555.

13 LOW PRICED HOLIDAY ACCOMMODATION

Dales Barns:
Barden Tower tel: (01756) 72016; Catholes Farm tel: (015396) 20334; Dub Cote Farm tel: (01729) 860238; Grange Farm tel: (01756) 760259; Skirfare Bridge tel: (01756) 752465; Hill Top Farm tel: (01729) 830320.

Youth Hostels:
Malham tel: (01729) 830321; Stainforth tel: (01729) 823577; Linton tel: (01756) 752400; Dent tel: (015396) 25251; Ingleton tel: (015242) 41444; Aysgarth tel: (01969) 663260; Kirkby Stephen tel: (017683) 71793; Grinton Lodge tel: (01748) 884206; Hawes tel: (01969) 667368; Keld tel: (01748) 886259; Kettlewell tel: (01756) 760232.

Further details from:
YHA Northern England Regional Office
PO Box 11, Matlock
Derbys DE4 2XA
Tel: (01629) 825850

Walk 1
SEDBERGH AND THE RIVER RAWTHEY
4½ miles (7.2 km) Easy/moderate

Even though the pleasant market town of Sedbergh is 'officially' part of the Yorkshire Dales National Park, it has an atmosphere more akin to the Lake District than those towns and villages of the eastern dales. Sheltered by the Howgill Fells to its north, Sedbergh has a sunny aspect and is fortunate in having the Rawthey, a fine trout river and a tributary of the Lune, on its doorstep. There are parking facilities in the town centre and access is via the A683 Kirkby Stephen road or the A684 from Wensleydale. From the M6, follow the A684 eastwards from Junction 37. This walk can be extended by joining it to Walk 14, which begins and ends in Sedbergh.

3 Bear right at Castlehaw Farm into open fields. Keep to the left of the boundary wall but change sides at a stile next to a massive upright stone within the wall.

4 Turn right at Ghyll Farm and walk down the concrete lane.

5 Bear left around Stone Hall, go through a gate, turn left again and follow a boundary wall downhill.

6 Follow the field path to the right of Hollin Hill Farm.

2 Turn left to follow a narrow lane opposite the converging road junction.

7 Bear right at the side of the large white house and then walk down its access drive.

1 From the car park, walk to the right along Main Street for about 80 yards (73 m), passing the Information Centre.

10 Cross the Garsdale road and continue to follow the riverbank. Turn right with the path and climb past a school building, then beside the rugby field into Sedbergh. The town centre is to the left.

8 Follow yellow waymarks to the left through the stockyard at Buckbank. Follow the hedge downhill to the road bridge.

9 Cross the road, climb the stile and follow the riverside path downstream.

A The double mound on the right is a Motte & Bailey, the remains of a stockade fort probably built in the 11th century.

B Viewpoint looking across the Rawthey Valley into Garsdale.

C Viewpoint. Frostow Fells are opposite above the confluence of Garsdale's Clough River and the Rawthey stream.

D Viewpoint. Sedbergh is to your left, backed by the mass of the Howgill Fells.

11

Walk 2
HELL GILL
4¾ miles (7.6 km) Moderate

The final upper limits of Wensleydale end in the wild, little-known moors of Mallerstang Common and the walk is in this region as far as Hell Gill on the boundary of North Yorkshire with Cumbria. To reach the start of the walk, drive north-west along the B6259 (Kirkby Stephen road) for about a mile (1.6 km) beyond the Moorcock Inn; there is limited roadside parking and there are lay-bys between Shotlock tunnel and the prominent forest at Lunds.

> **5** *Cross the bridge and turn left, down the farm track. Cross the railway bridge and continue to the road.*

> **4** *Climb a stone stile and turn left along the moorland track.*

> **2** *Follow a signposted footpath to Shaws, the tree-sheltered white house high on the hillside.*

The High Way

Hell Gill Bridge

Hellgill

> **3** *Turn left over the bridge. Then bear right above the house. Follow a faint path up the hillside.*

> **9** *Keep above the portal of Shotlock tunnel. Go through the gate and turn right along the road.*

> **8** *Keep level across the pathless moor for about ¼ mile (402 m). Then descend gradually to the left, towards the railway tunnel.*

Shaws

Shotlock Tunnel

The Quarry

Aisgill Moor Cottages

High Shaw Paddock

> **6** *Cross the road. Then go through a gate and turn left. There is no path, so follow the moorland boundary wall.*

> **7** *Go half right through the abandoned farm-yard and, still following the boundary wall, aim for the gate in the corner of the next field.*

> **1** *Walk down the road, away from the forest, to a footpath sign near the Quarry. Turn left across a rough field and go through the pine wood. Turn right along the forest drive.*

A The abandoned simple stone chapel, to the right of the path, once served this scattered moorland community.

B Shaws stands above a narrow ravine filled by an attractive natural water garden.

C The track is an old coach road called the High Way which formerly linked York and Carlisle. The track mostly follows the north side of Wensleydale and, in places, it is difficult to trace but, in its lower reaches below Askrigg, it is now the basis of the modern road.

D Viewpoint. The moors of Mallerstang Common are opposite; Wild Boar Fell is the highest point – 2323 feet (708 m) – and Aisgill waterfall can usually be seen close to the railway line.

E Sturdy Hell Gill Bridge was built to last, once carrying coaches and horses as well as driven cattle. Look over the parapet on either side into the deep chasm created by the stream wearing its way through a section of softer limestone.

F Aisgill summit is the highest point on the Settle to Carlisle line, where steam trains are run frequently.

Walk 3
KISDON HILL
4¼ miles (6.8 km) Moderate

Kisdon Hill's grassy bulk dominates the head of Swaledale and its circuit offers a high-level panoramic ramble, with delightful views of the surrounding heather moors. The walk is from Keld, the highest village in the dale, and is approached by a side road off the B6270. Park in the village but take care not to block access to private property. The name Keld is the modern version of Kelda, which is Old Norse for a spring. Following the decline of lead mining in the late 19th century, the village lost the major portion of its population and has never recovered.

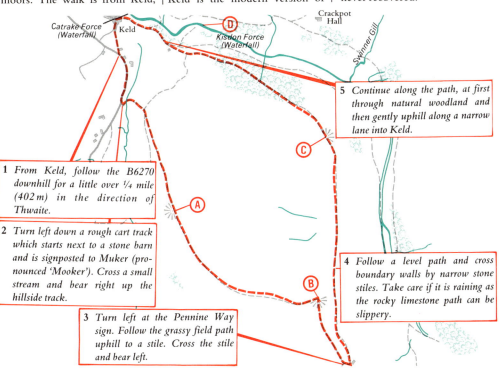

1 From Keld, follow the B6270 downhill for a little over ¼ mile (402 m) in the direction of Thwaite.

2 Turn left down a rough cart track which starts next to a stone barn and is signposted to Muker (pronounced 'Mooker'). Cross a small stream and bear right up the hillside track.

3 Turn left at the Pennine Way sign. Follow the grassy field path uphill to a stile. Cross the stile and bear left.

4 Follow a level path and cross boundary walls by narrow stone stiles. Take care if it is raining as the rocky limestone path can be slippery.

5 Continue along the path, at first through natural woodland and then gently uphill along a narrow lane into Keld.

A Viewpoint. The complex field patterns with their tiny stone barns are a typical feature of Upper Swaledale. Angram, a cluster of roadside farms, is directly across the valley.

B Viewpoint. This is considered by many to be one of the finest views in the Yorkshire Dales. Swaledale cuts a deep lush swathe through the rolling heather moors. Muker is directly below – a cluster of snug houses and farms in this exposed valley.

C Viewpoint. Swinner Gill, a one-time area of intensive lead mining, is opposite. Crackpot Hall is to the left of the deep-cut valley, ruined since rival interests undermined its foundations.

D Attractive waterfalls are another feature of Upper Swaledale. A signposted path, to the right of the walk, leads down to Kisdon Force. Closer to Keld, East Gill Force is in a pretty tree-lined hollow. Catrake, Currack and Wain Wath Forces are upstream from the village on either side of Park Bridge.

13

Walk 4
CAM ROAD AND THE PENNINE WAY
6 miles (9.7 km) Moderate/strenuous; one climb of 1116 feet (340 m)

Two ancient tracks which converge on Hawes are followed by this walk. The first, Cam Road, is an old drove road, one of the many green roads which crisscross the Yorkshire Dales. No longer used for transporting cattle and sheep to Midland markets, it now serves as a convenient track for local farmers to reach the high moorland pastures as well as being a pleasant walker's path. The second is a delightful grassy track now followed by the Pennine Way long-distance footpath. Originally, the path was a more direct link between Cam Road and Hawes. It was also used as an access track to reach the peat-gathering grounds at Ten End. Ten End is the junction point for both tracks and the inward turning point for the walk. Car parking should be easy to find at either end of Hawes.

Hawes is a busy market town, the 'capital' of Upper Wharfedale and a useful base for exploring the dales to the north. The word Hawes comes from a Norse word 'haus', meaning a pass or gap. It is sometimes corrupted as 'house', and occurs throughout the Northern Pennines and the Lake District. Hawes no longer has a railway but the old station buildings have been put to good use as the Yorkshire Dales National Park Information Centre and also the Upper Dales Folk Museum. The latter houses a collection of farm equipment and records of the area's past, made by two Daleswomen. At one time, hand knitting was an important secondary industry to farming but the only remaining traditional hand craft in Wensleydale is rope-

making. In a shed at the entrance to the station car park, the 200-year-old method of hand twisting short ropes is demonstrated. The ropes are used for cattle or horse halters. The famous Wensleydale cheese is made at the nearby dairy, to traditionally high standards but by modern methods.

Before starting out on the walk, look at the plaque above the door of the house opposite the telephone kiosks. Obviously strong supporters of the Commonwealth which followed the Civil War, the original owners ask the unanswerable question:

'God being with us
who can be against?'

The date over the plaque is 1668 but we do not know who built the house, other than his initials, which were T.A.F.

A Cam Road. This is one of the 'green roads' which have crisscrossed the Dales since time immemorial. Cam Road is a link with Cam High Road which it joins in the south-west at Kidhow Gate. Cam High Road is Roman in origin and can be traced from Ingleton to Bainbridge. Parts of its surface are metalled but, as with Cam Road, it runs for miles across the moors as a high-level track. Once used by drovers and local travellers, the track is freely available to walkers and horse riders.

B Viewpoint. The little side dale

of Snaizeholme Beck is below and the bold outline of Ingleborough rises beyond the dale head.

C The path, from Ten End, is part of the 270-mile (435 km) Pennine Way footpath which links Edale in Derbyshire with Kirk Yetholm in the Scottish Borders. Even though the moorland path is easy to follow at this point, prominent cairns also indicate its route.

D Viewpoint. Wensleydale is below. The Pennine Way crosses the dale beyond Hawes and climbs the broad shoulder of

Great Shunner Fell away to your left.

E Viewpoint. Gayle, the village in front and to the right, is worth a few minutes diversion. Attractive cottages line the roads on either side of the stepped waterfalls of Gayle Beck. The village was founded by Vikings who built on the foundations of a Celtic settlement.

F Notice the curious little spire which has been added, almost as an afterthought, to one corner of the tower of Hawes church.

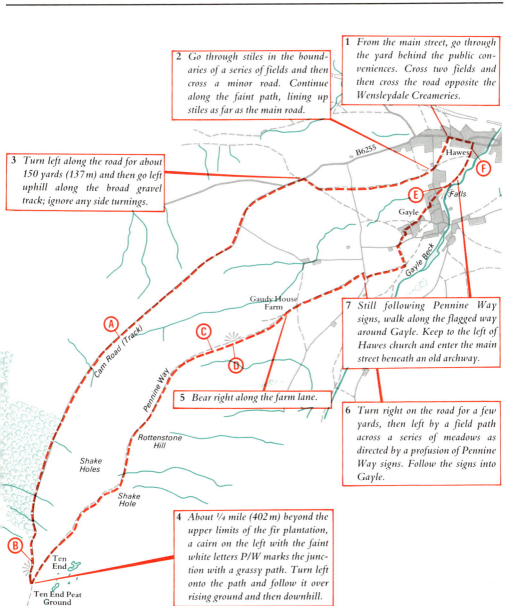

2 Go through stiles in the boundaries of a series of fields and then cross a minor road. Continue along the faint path, lining up stiles as far as the main road.

1 From the main street, go through the yard behind the public conveniences. Cross two fields and then cross the road opposite the Wensleydale Creameries.

3 Turn left along the road for about 150 yards (137 m) and then go left uphill along the broad gravel track; ignore any side turnings.

7 Still following Pennine Way signs, walk along the flagged way around Gayle. Keep to the left of Hawes church and enter the main street beneath an old archway.

5 Bear right along the farm lane.

6 Turn right on the road for a few yards, then left by a field path across a series of meadows as directed by a profusion of Pennine Way signs. Follow the signs into Gayle.

4 About ¼ mile (402 m) beyond the upper limits of the fir plantation, a cairn on the left with the faint white letters P/W marks the junction with a grassy path. Turn left onto the path and follow it over rising ground and then downhill.

15

Walk 5
MIDDLEHAM
2½ miles (4km) Easy

Richard, Duke of Gloucester, Yorkist and future King Richard III (1452-1485), once lived in the imposing Norman Castle which still dominates Middleham. The small market town is at the junction of the A6108, Leyburn road and the minor road which runs along Coverdale to Kettlewell in Wharfedale. To join the walk, park near the market square.

The main walls of the castle date from 1170 when it became the property of the powerful Neville family but the massive and well-preserved Keep is the original, built by Robert Fitzralf, nephew of William the Conqueror. Its towering bulk remains a true memorial to the master masons who erected it more than eight centuries ago. The white boar crest of the hunchbacked King Richard can (with a little imagination) still be made out on top of the Swine Cross in the market square.

Another feature in the town is St. Alkelda's Well, the martyred Saxon princess who died at the hands of the Danes rather than renounce her Christian beliefs. It is her name to which the parish church is dedicated. In the market place and near the Swine Cross, there is a ring where bulls were once tied for the cruel sport of bull-baiting.

During his training to become a knight, Richard met and married Anne, the daughter of Richard Neville who was better known as Warwick the Kingmaker. Through Anne, he became owner of Middleham and spent many happy hours indulging in the royal sport of hunting game throughout the Dales. Edward, Richard's only legitimate son, was born in Middleham but died aged 12. His room can be seen in the castle ruins. King Richard, since his portrayal by Shakespeare in Richard III, has been looked upon as an evil king but recent research sees him otherwise. It is in this light that we can think of him as a lover of the Dales, especially Coverdale and his beloved Middleham Castle.

Middleham, the Newmarket of the North, is the centre of a bloodstock breeding area with a dozen or so trainers handling hundreds of potentially top-class racehorses. These fine animals are exercised on the wide expanse of Middleham Moor, to the north of the Coverdale road.

About a mile (1.6km) beyond Middleham towards Leyburn, the road crosses the River Ure by an imposing iron girder bridge, which was built by public subscription in 1850, replacing a suspension bridge which collapsed in 1831 after only two years' use. Below the town, in Swaledale, the River Ure, which is now joined by the Cover, widens as it reaches the broad acres of the Vale of York. The dale's character becomes more wooded in its flatter lower reaches. About 3 miles (4.8km) from Middleham along the Masham Road, you will find the ruins of Jervaulx Abbey. During the life of this abbey, the Cistercian monks who lived there became famous for their cheese, a forerunner of Wensleydale, but made from ewes' milk.

In 1536, the Pilgrimage of Grace started from Jervaulx, led by the abbot, Adam Sedbergh. His intention was to try to persuade Henry VIII against the dissolution of the monasteries but the pilgrimage failed and Jervaulx, along with countless others, was destroyed. Abbot Sedbergh and many of his followers were imprisoned in the Tower of London and executed at Tyburn in 1537.

A The imposing ruins of the castle are worth viewing from within and also from the lane end. When Richard III, having reigned for only two years, lost not only his horse and the Battle of Bosworth but also the Crown of England in 1485, his successor, Henry Tudor, had no wish to own Middleham. Along with the unhappy memories of his rival, it was abandoned and languished for 161 years. However, because it retained its obvious potential as a fortress, Cromwell's troops made it untenable in 1646, during the Civil War. Its ruins later became a free quarry for ready-dressed stones and many of the older houses in the town are probably built from materials

taken from the castle. The castle is now in the care of English Heritage.

B A mound which tops the rising field on the right predates the castle and is the earth base of an earlier timber fortification which was abandoned when the main castle was built.

C Hullo Bridge. Its stone arch speaks of its use by once heavier traffic than cattle or the occasional tractor and probably carried a coach road south across Coverdale to the interesting 17th-century house of Braithwaite Hall Parts of the two riverside fields south of Hullo Bridge are available for picnicking or strolling under the 'Countryside Stewardship' scheme.

D The attractive pond on the left is a popular picnic spot. Horses can often be seen being exercised on the nearby common

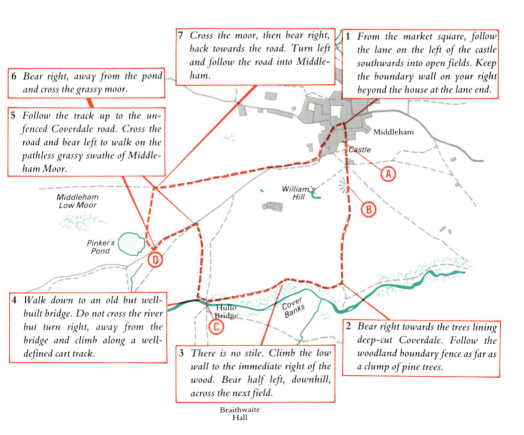

7 Cross the moor, then bear right, back towards the road. Turn left and follow the road into Middleham.

1 From the market square, follow the lane on the left of the castle southwards into open fields. Keep the boundary wall on your right beyond the house at the lane end.

6 Bear right, away from the pond and cross the grassy moor.

5 Follow the track up to the unfenced Coverdale road. Cross the road and bear left to walk on the pathless grassy swathe of Middleham Moor.

Middleham

Castle

A

William's Hill

B

Middleham Low Moor

Pinker's Pond

D

4 Walk down to an old but wellbuilt bridge. Do not cross the river but turn right, away from the bridge and climb along a welldefined cart track.

Hullo Bridge

Cover Banks

C

2 Bear right towards the trees lining deep-cut Coverdale. Follow the woodland boundary fence as far as a clump of pine trees.

3 There is no stile. Climb the low wall to the immediate right of the wood. Bear half left, downhill, across the next field.

Braithwaite Hall

17

Walk 6
INGLETON'S WATERFALLS

4½ miles (7.2 km) Moderate, slippery areas when wet; one climb of 500 feet (152 m)

This is probably the most beautiful walk in the Yorkshire Dales. For most of the way, the footpath is privately owned and, as a result, a small admission fee is charged, but this will be of little consequence when balanced against the privilege of walking in such delightful surroundings.

Two rivers, the Doe and Twiss, join below Ingleton to become the Greta, itself a tributary of the Lune, one of the two Dales' rivers flowing into the Irish Sea (the other is the Ribble). Upstream from Ingleton, the Doe and Twiss, after their birth on the opposite side of Whernside, flow through flat-bottomed upper valleys before cascading down tree-lined limestone gorges. The walk follows their course in a clock-

wise direction, upstream along the Twiss, then down the Doe.

Much of the geology of the Ingleton area is revealed by the rivers' flow. Around the car park, the underlying rock is mostly shale and slate, which accounts for the comparatively flat land to the west. Harder slates form the river-bed upstream for most of the way and the more easily eroded limestones have been worn into glens and gorges where natural amphitheatres are slowly being cut back under the force of their waterfalls. Above the narrowest of these gorges, further slate deposits resist the downward action of the rivers, making their course more gentle. In the higher parts of the upper dale, where the main limestone beds

are found, any water soon disappears underground, not emerging until it meets the impervious lower slate beds.

Spring is the best time to appreciate the walk, when the water levels of both rivers are still fairly high and the delicate green of newly leafed trees form a backcloth but don't screen the views of the deeper ravines.

Parking and refreshments are available at the beginning of the walk. Approach the car park by driving through Ingleton from either the A65 Settle road or the B6255 Hawes road and then follow the side road steeply down into the valley. Access to the car park is well signposted from the village.

A The outward section of the walk follows the River Twiss upstream. Its waterfalls tend to be wider than the Doe's and are best seen face on. Those of the Doe are mostly in tree-lined narrow ravines, which are more dramatic when viewed from above. Both rivers join a few yards below the road which leads into the car park.

B Pecca Falls, a series of narrow cascades. There is usually a hut open on the nearby hillside, where refreshments are on sale.

C Thornton Force. The highest

waterfall — 46 feet (14 m) — in the Ingleton area and, scenically, the most attractive. The tree-fringed limestone crag makes a natural amphitheatre. The darker rock beneath the falls is slate which, unlike limestone, is impervious to water.

D Beezley Falls. The first cascade of the hitherto peaceful River Doe. The river's other name is the Greta, a title which is retained by the main river below Ingleton. Outcrops and boulders in the river-bed cause the stream to make several dramatic changes of its direction.

E Snow Falls. One of a series of three in the section of the valley known as Twistleton Glen.

F The quarry, here, once exploited the harder but more easily worked slate which forms the bed-rock of this normally limestone region.

G Cat Leap Fall. A little off route, on the left, this fall is the final exuberant act of Skirwith Beck, a side stream which joins the Doe close by an old limestone quarry.

Walk 6
Ingleton's Waterfalls
continued

0   1 mile

0   1 km

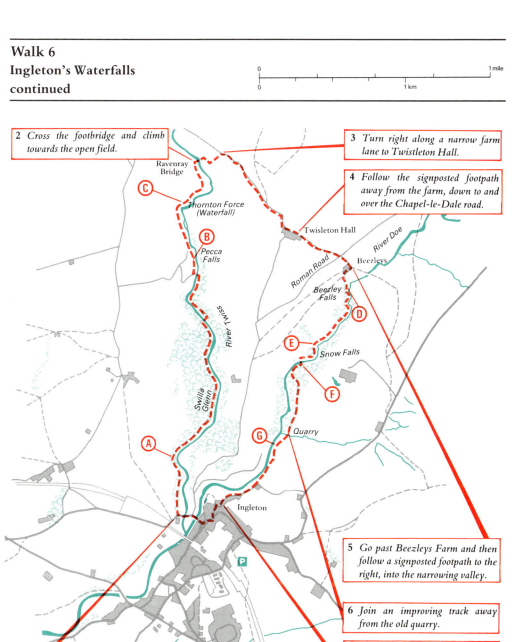

2 *Cross the footbridge and climb towards the open field.*

3 *Turn right along a narrow farm lane to Twistleton Hall.*

4 *Follow the signposted footpath away from the farm, down to and over the Chapel-le-Dale road.*

Ravenray Bridge

Thornton Force (Waterfall)

Pecca Falls

Twisleton Hall

Beezleys

Roman Road

River Doe

Beezley Falls

River Twiss

Snow Falls

Swilla Glenn

Quarry

Ingleton

P

5 *Go past Beezleys Farm and then follow a signposted footpath to the right, into the narrowing valley.*

6 *Join an improving track away from the old quarry.*

7 *Bear left into the centre of Ingleton, past the church and then turn right, down the road to the car park.*

1 *Follow the wide footpath away from the car park, upstream through tree-lined Swilla Glen.*

Walk 7
CAM END AND LING GILL
6¼ miles (10 km) Moderate/strenuous; one climb of 390 feet (119 m)

Here is a walk to link short stretches of the Dales Way and the Pennine Way. The section which follows the Dales Way from Gearstones uses part of the Roman road from Lancaster to Bainbridge. It joins the Pennine Way at Cam End – a green road used originally as a drove road but now used by Pennine Wayfar-ers. For the return to Gearstones, this track will lead you down past Ling Gill to Old Ing Farm where farm tracks and footpaths cross the moors.

Parking is limited around the farm settlement of Gearstones. Be careful not to block access to farm entrances or field gates. The large building in the middle of the group was once an inn, used by Scottish drovers moving the half wild black Galloway cattle to southern markets. The house stands at the side of the B6255 Ribblehead to Hawes road about 1½ miles (2.4 km) north-east of the viaduct.

A Gearstones Lodge. A building has stood on the site for centuries. It was once an inn giving accommodation to cattle drovers who passed this way south along Cam High Road. The track was linked in its turn to other roads and trackways to the north and south; some are now metalled roads but others have almost disappeared.

B A signpost will indicate that the track is part of the Dales Way. Its foundations are Roman, although nothing remains of the original road other than the route.

C Low circular stone and turf walls on the left of the track could be mistaken for prehistoric relics but they are, in fact, modern shooting butts. Red grouse, the target of sportsmen in late summer and autumn, give themselves away by their low, erratic flight patterns and cries of 'ge-beck, ge-beck'.

D The track is now part of the Horton to Hawes section of the Pennine Way.

E Viewpoint. The Three Peaks can be seen from this point. From left to right are Penyghent, Ingleborough and Whernside, the latter two towering above Ribblehead viaduct. The circuit of these steep mountains is a hard day's expedition for most walkers but fell runners manage to complete the race in a few hours.

F Ling Gill Bridge. A plaque set into the upstream parapet of the bridge tells us that in 1765 it was repaired at 'the charge of the whole West Rideing (sic)', an indication of its once greater importance.

G Ling Gill National Nature Reserve. The limestone gorge on the right is filled with woodland, the remnant of forests which once covered much of the limestone dales. It is possible to enter Ling Gill to examine the plants at close quarters but on no account may any be taken without a permit from the Regional Controller, Most of the gill can be seen from the track but if you go into the reserve, take great care on the slippery edge of the ravine.

H Calf Holes. A pothole is over the wall on the left, at the start of the double walled section of the track. Water cascading into its depths reappears about ½ a mile (0.8 km) away to the north-west at Browgill Cave.

I God's Bridge. A wide natural arch formed by Blow Gill Beck tunnelling through a weakness in the limestone surface rocks.

J Viewpoint. The deep-cut little valley to the south-west is Thorns Gill, an unspoilt natural habitat for wild flowers in its wooded lower reaches, ½ a mile (0.8 km) downstream. Ingleborough, Ribblehead Viaduct and Whernside can be glimpsed from the slopes leading down to the footbridge.

Walk 7
Cam End and Ling Gill
continued

1 *Follow the main road north-east from Gearstones.*

2 *Turn right, away from the road, out onto a wide moorland track. Cross Gayle Beck by a footbridge and climb steadily.*

3 *Turn right at the wooden signpost and continue downhill along a wide track.*

11 *Cross the footbridge and climb the stile opposite. Walk up the field and go to the left of the largest building to join the B6255.*

10 *Bear right at the abandoned farm buildings at Thorns. Follow the boundary wall over the open moor.*

4 *Cross Ling Gill Bridge and bear right, along a rocky track.*

9 *Go through the gate next to a stone barn and turn right. Follow the boundary wall uphill and across two fields.*

8 *Go through the farm-yard at Nether Lodge and follow the signpost pointing to Gearstones. There is no path across the rough grassy moor but a stile and two gates show the way.*

7 *Continue ahead on a grassy path and follow the wall where the broader track turns right.*

5 *Bear half right, through a gate and go down the farm lane away from the Pennine Way.*

6 *Turn right at the signpost to Nether Lodge. Follow the field track above the wooded valley.*

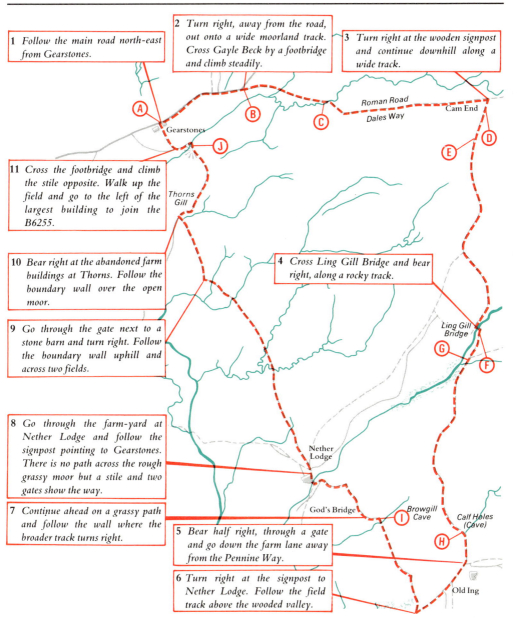

21

Walk 8
HORTON IN RIBBLESDALE
5 miles (8km) Easy

0   1 mile

0   1 km

This walk follows the Ribble from Horton in Ribblesdale, a popular village on the B6479 Settle to Ribblehead road. A riverside stroll is followed by a gentle uphill ramble through fields which, in turn, leads to quiet byways surrounding Horton.

1 *From the car park in Horton in Ribblesdale, cross the footbridge and turn left on a field path, away from the road. Follow the riverbank downstream.*

2 *Avoid a wide bend in the river by turning right as directed by a signpost. Cross the field and join a sunken lane.*

3 *Cross the river by the footbridge and bear left over the fields using stiles in their walls. Turn left along the road.*

4 *Turn right and follow the side road as far as a barn near the next junction with the main road. Follow the signpost on the right to Dub Cote. There is no path but keep to the right of a second barn and then left over the stile.*

5 *Climb two adjacent fields, crossing a ladder stile over their boundary wall. Keep to the left of White Sike Barn and then turn right along a walled track.*

6 *Go to the right along the road, uphill past Brackenbottom Farm and then downhill by the side of Douk Ghyll.*

7 *Turn right, cross the stream by a footbridge and then turn right again. Follow the lane signposted 'Pennine Way'.*

8 *Turn left at the lane junction, downhill into Horton. The main car park is to the right along the road.*

River Ribble

Horton in Ribblesdale

Brackenbottom

Horton Bridge

Dub Cote

White Sike Barn

Studfold

A Viewpoint. A log bridge spanning the Ribble makes an interesting foreground to the view of Penyghent. The river is an excellent trout stream where visiting and resident birds take advantage of the unspoilt environment of its quiet banks.

B Viewpoint. You can see Horton and the Upper Ribble Valley with the eastern slopes of Ingleborough to the far left.

C Dub Cote Bunk House. This is one of several redundant barns throughout the Yorkshire Dales, which have been converted into simple accommodation. For further details, tel: (01729) 8602380.

Walk 9
ATTERMIRE SCAR

5 miles (8 km) Moderate/strenuous; total climb of 700 feet (213 m)

The walk starts from the centre of Settle, 'capital' of Upper Ribblesdale. This is a busy market town on the A65 and there are parking facilities near the market place. Settle is also the southern terminus of the scenic Settle to Carlisle railway. Soon after leaving the bustle of the town, steep but easy-to-follow paths climb to the limestone wilderness of Attermire Scar. Several small caves penetrate its craggy lower slopes. A torch is desirable if you plan to explore their depths. The return is by a gently descending field track with wide-ranging views of Ribblesdale and the Craven district.

6 *At the point where the track joins the road, turn left through a small gate and follow a field path along the bottom edge of a mature wood.*

5 *Turn left through a metal gate and follow the well-made farm track downhill.*

7 *Use the gate in the narrow gap between two sections of woodland.*

8 *Take the stile at the side of the wicket gate. Walk ahead along a field path and descend by an improving track into the outskirts of Settle.*

2 *Bear right, away from the road and follow the rough-walled lane uphill.*

3 *About 100 yards (91 m) beyond a clump of trees, turn right at a signpost to Malham. Climb the grassy hillside. At first, there is no path but one soon develops. Follow this to the right of the boundary wall.*

4 *Cross two stiles and then go through a gap in the wall. Turn left and climb the rocky path along the foot of the crags.*

1 *Follow the road to the left of the market place and climb towards Constitution Hill.*

Map labels: Jubilee Cave, Victoria Cave, Brent Scar, Attermire Scar, Warrendale Knotts, Caves, Horseshoe Cave, Langcliffe, Settle

A Viewpoint across the townscape of Settle and the Ribble Valley with the Ingleborough fells on the right.

B Viewpoint. The limestone crags of Attermire Scar, the surface indication of the line of a major geological fault, fill the steep hillside on your left giving it the appearance of a much higher mountain. Malham Moor is directly ahead.

C The caves of Attermire Scar. Attermire Cave is above direction pointer 4 and four small caves surround Victoria Cave near the highest point of the climb. Jubilee Cave, so named because of its discovery at the time of Queen Victoria's Jubilee, is about 110 yards (101 m) uphill beyond pointer no.5. Traces of habitation from pre-historic to post-Roman times have been found in some of the caves.

Walk 10
UPPER LITTONDALE
4 miles (6.4 km) Moderate

Wild Upper Littondale is one of the least visited places in the Dales. A tributary of Wharfedale, its stark moorland solitude contrasts with more popular areas. The valley road leaves the B6160 at Skirfare Bridge between Kettlewell and Kilnsey and makes a sharp left turn at Halton Gill to climb beneath Penyghent on its way to Stainforth. A short cul-de-sac road from Halton Gill continues for about a mile to Foxup and it is from here that the walk starts. Roadside parking is limited but a few spaces can usually be found near Foxup Bridge.

6 *Cross the road to the left of Halton Gill Bridge. Continue by riverside field path back to Foxup Bridge.*

1 *Turn left opposite Foxup Bridge Farm and go through a gate. Climb the grassy track signposted to Horton in Ribblesdale.*

2 *Bear left, away from the wall as indicated by a signpost. There is no clear path but the route is marked by blue-topped posts.*

3 *Turn right along the metalled road and follow it for about ⅓ of a mile (536 m).*

4 *Turn sharp left at a signpost and follow a wire fence diagonally downhill to Nether Heselden Farm.*

5 *Go through the farm-yard and turn left, then go through a gate at the side of a large circular slurry tank. Follow the signposted route across a series of fields.*

Foxup
Foxup Beck
Halton Gill
Halton Gill Bridge
Berghle (Pot Hole)
Calena Pot
Red Dot Pots
Littondale
River Skirfare
Flamethrower Hole
Settlement & Field System
Hesleden
Penyghent Gill

A Notice how the sturdy farmhouses at Foxup turn their backs to the cold north wind.

B Viewpoint. Looking down Littondale towards Wharfedale in the hazy distance.

C Viewpoint. Penyghent can be seen ahead with Fountains Fell on the left.

D Viewpoint. The deep ravine of Penyghent Gill is on the right. The trees along the river-bank are remnants of forests which covered the Dales before the last Ice Age.

24

Walk 11
THE WATERFALLS OF AYSGARTH AND WEST BURTON
4¾ miles (7.6 km) Easy

0 _____ 1 mile
0 _____ 1 km

West Burton is a little over a mile (1.6 km) to the south of Aysgarth. A series of waterfalls fills the tiny gorge below West Burton and, although just as attractive as their more famous sisters on either side of Aysgarth's mill bridge, these falls are almost unknown. This walk visits both sets of falls and provides the opportunity of comparing their merits. From the National Park car park north of the bridge, the walk is through fields to West Burton, then back via a footpath along the south bank and less frequented section of the Ure.

To reach the car park and Information Centre at Aysgarth, leave the A684 by driving down the Carperby road.

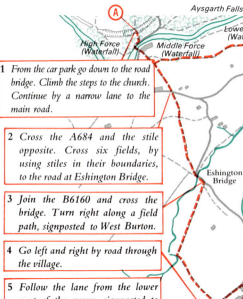

1 *From the car park go down to the road bridge. Climb the steps to the church. Continue by a narrow lane to the main road.*

2 *Cross the A684 and the stile opposite. Cross six fields, by using stiles in their boundaries, to the road at Eshington Bridge.*

3 *Join the B6160 and cross the bridge. Turn right along a field path, signposted to West Burton.*

4 *Go left and right by road through the village.*

5 *Follow the lane from the lower part of the green, signposted to The Waterfall. Cross the narrow stone bridge. Then, by path, go left and right uphill.*

6 *Continue ahead as signposted to Barrack Wood, then left by woodland path.*

7 *Turn left down the farm lane and then right by a field path signposted to Edgley. Waymarked stiles and gates mark the route.*

8 *Turn right along the road for about 130 yards (120 m), then left through a gate into the last field on the left. Go diagonally across the field to the main road.*

9 *Turn left over Hestholme Bridge and right by a waymarked path on its far side. Follow the river-bank to Aysgarth church.*

A Before the walk, you can follow the nature trail to the Middle and Lower Falls. Access to the falls is signposted from the car park. Also visit the Carriage Museum in the Old Corn Mill. High Force is upstream of the mill bridge. Spring is the time for this walk, especially after heavy rain when the woods and flowers are at their best and the falls at their most spectacular.

B West Burton is built around a wide village green. You can still see the smithy and the Fox & Hounds Inn is to the right of the renovated stocks. A curious spire takes the place of a more conventional preaching cross.

C Viewpoint. West Burton's waterfall from the footbridge.

D Twin stone follies on higher ground, off the path to the right, were built by lead miners around 1860. One looks like a pepper pot and was used for smoking bacon.

E Viewpoint. Lower and Middle Falls in their woodland setting.

Walk 12
HAWKSWICK MOOR
7 miles (11.3 km) Moderate/strenuous

Footpaths, which are centuries old, are used to connect the three villages and two dales visited on this walk. The paths date from a time long before roads designed to cope with wheeled traffic appeared in the Dales, a time when most people rarely travelled beyond their parish boundaries.

The first village, the point of departure for the walk, is Kettlewell in Wharfedale; the name is Old Norse and its meaning is either 'Kettil's Well', or 'Bubbling Spring'. Beyond Knife Scar, the path descends into Littondale. This name differs from most of the other dales, except Wensleydale, in that it is not derived from the name of the river. In this case, the river is the Skirfare. Hawkswick is the next village, its name indicating that birds of prey once lived nearby. Arncliffe village also has similar links: although its name has no immediate apparent meaning, in translation from Old Norse, it means Eagles' Cliff.

Charles Kingsley stayed for a time in Arncliffe, when he was writing his novel, 'The Water Babies', a book which condemned the Victorian practice of sending small boys up chimneys in order to sweep down the soot. He travelled widely throughout the Yorkshire Dales and his water babies' home was the pool at the foot of Malham Cove.

Park your car in Kettlewell. There is usually space near the bridge or along one of the village streets but be careful not to interfere with access to premises or block farm gates.

A Viewpoint. Look back towards Kettlewell. Its church is unusual in that it is built to one side of the village, rather than near the centre, inferring, perhaps, that the village has expanded westwards rather than outwards from a central point. The main road only touches the outskirts of the village. Most of the old cottages lining the side streets and alleys were once the homes of lead miners who worked beneath the nearby fells. Kettlewell was an important halt in the days of coaches and horses; its three inns date from that time. The main route from London to Richmond followed Wensleydale to Kettlewell, then climbed over the notoriously steep Park Rash to the north-east of the village, where passengers were expected to get out and push! Park Rash has been used as a hill-climb to test cars and motor-cycles.

B Viewpoint. Pastoral Wharfedale is ahead and contrasts with rockier and narrower Littondale to your right. Immediately below are the rough outlines of a prehistoric field system. People were able to live on these higher fells during a period when the climate was warmer than now.

C Viewpoint. Hawkswick and its sheltering belt of trees is below. The Skirfare flows gently by the village on its way to join the Wharfe at Amerdale Dub. Dubs are deep pools in rivers, usually the home of large trout.

D The route passes Arncliffe church. The rest of the village is to the left. It has one pub, the Falcon, and a tea room.

E Primroses, bluebells and woodland violets grow in profusion every spring in Park Scar woods. Please leave them where they are: picking wild flowers spoils the enjoyment of other visitors and also it will often kill the parent plant.

F Viewpoint. Arncliffe is below amidst its ancient field patterns outlined by enclosure walls.

G Heather growing on the rocky fellside indicates that the soil is acidic and the surface rock is gritstone, capping the more common Dales' limestone, which is an alkaline rock. Native heather will only grow in an acid environment.

H Viewpoint. Kettlewell is framed in the lower portals of the rocky cleft in Gate Close Scar. Take care when following the path over its slippery rocks.

7 Climb the steep footpath signposted to Kettlewell. Go through a belt of mature woodland below the escarpment rocks.

8 The moorland path is indistinct in places. Look for a prominent signpost on the skyline pointing the way to the right, towards a clearer track.

9 Cross a well-defined cart track and continue downhill diagonally across the hillside on a grassy path. Go down a narrow rocky gully to reach the valley bottom.

10 Go through a gate and turn left at the road. Cross the bridge into Kettlewell village.

1 Follow the Threshfield road (B6160) out of Kettlewell for a little over a quarter of a mile (402 m). Turn right through a gate marked by a signpost to Hawkswick. Climb the rocky path across the sparsely wooded hillside.

2 Yellow waymarks indicate the route of the hillside path which becomes grassier as it gains height.

Arncliffe

Hawkswick Moor

Kettlewell

Hawkswick

River Wharfe

6 Cross the road bridge and immediately turn right across a small meadow to reach the minor road. Cross it diagonally right to a stile.

5 Bear left, temporarily away from the river. Follow waymarks and stiles slightly uphill to rejoin the river-bank.

4 Turn left across a narrow metal footbridge, then right on a field path. Follow the river upstream.

3 Follow the road to the right through Hawkswick.

27

Walk 13
GHAISTRILL'S STRID AND GRASS WOOD
4¼ miles (7.2 km) Easy/moderate

This walk is from Grassington, 'capital' of the Dales and headquarters of the Yorkshire Dales National Park, the body entrusted with the difficult task of preserving and enhancing the landscape, as well as protecting the livelihoods of people living and working within the boundaries of the park. The authority must also look after the amenity interests of the thousands of visitors who wish to enjoy this part of the English countryside.

Grassington is a small town with a mixture of architectural styles, including many fine Georgian dwellings, and, although it grew with the fortunes of nearby lead mines, its foundations are much older. The town suffered during the period of Scottish border raids in the 14th and later centuries but worse by far was the visitation of the Black Death plague in 1349, when over a quarter of the population in the vicinity of Grassington died.

The Upper Wharfedale Folk Museum of farming and local industry is in the town square. Adventure holidays and caving and climbing training courses are organised by the Dales Centre which is also based in Grassington. There are two car parks in Grassington. The largest is near the Information Centre off the Pateley Bridge, B6265, road.

A Ghaistrill's Strid. An attractive picnic site next to a narrow river channel of strangely carved limestone rocks. Do not attempt to jump the Strid (Stride): the Wharfe flows deep and fast.

B Grass Wood Nature Reserve is owned and maintained by the Yorkshire Naturalists Trust. Visitors are allowed to use the right of way through the wood but are expected to observe a few simple rules and respect the wildlife of this unique woodland habitat. Many varieties of spring flowers, including lily of the valley and much rarer plants, bloom in Grass Wood. Please do not pick any of them as it often kills the parent plant.

C Viewpoint. Dramatic Kilnsey Crag can be seen about 1¼ miles (2 km) to the north-west, upstream, of this point. The crag is a popular climbing area for rock gymnasts but the less energetic can enjoy the amenities of the Kilnsey Trout Farm and nearby angling pools.

D Viewpoint. Trees have overgrown the ancient settlement but many of its substantial walls can still be traced. Here is an old village which predates Georgian Grassington and was built across what was once an open treeless hillside. The Black Death wiped out most of its inhabitants and the farms and houses were abandoned to nature. Beautiful Grass Wood now covers a scene of sickness and tragedy.

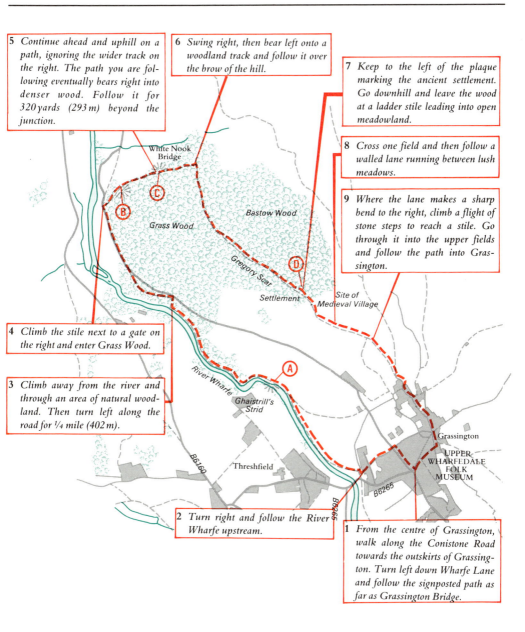

5 Continue ahead and uphill on a path, ignoring the wider track on the right. The path you are following eventually bears right into denser wood. Follow it for 320 yards (293 m) beyond the junction.

6 Swing right, then bear left onto a woodland track and follow it over the brow of the hill.

7 Keep to the left of the plaque marking the ancient settlement. Go downhill and leave the wood at a ladder stile leading into open meadowland.

8 Cross one field and then follow a walled lane running between lush meadows.

9 Where the lane makes a sharp bend to the right, climb a flight of stone steps to reach a stile. Go through it into the upper fields and follow the path into Grassington.

4 Climb the stile next to a gate on the right and enter Grass Wood.

3 Climb away from the river and through an area of natural woodland. Then turn left along the road for ¼ mile (402 m).

2 Turn right and follow the River Wharfe upstream.

1 From the centre of Grassington, walk along the Conistone Road towards the outskirts of Grassington. Turn left down Wharfe Lane and follow the signposted path as far as Grassington Bridge.

White Nook Bridge

Grass Wood

Bastow Wood

Gregory Scar

Settlement

Site of Medieval Village

River Wharfe

Ghaistrill's Strid

B6160

Threshfield

B6265

B6265

Grassington

UPPER WHARFEDALE FOLK MUSEUM

Walk 14
GARGRAVE
7½ miles (12 km) Easy, muddy sections after rain

Gargrave is just outside the southern boundary of the Yorkshire Dales National Park and also marks the boundary between the Yorkshire Dales and Craven, a district of lush pastures on land made from the debris left by a retreating ice sheet. As a one-time coaching village, Gargrave's links with these bygone traditions are maintained by a number of hospitable roadside inns which remind travellers on the modern A65 of more leisurely modes of transport.

Strategically placed in a central position within the Aire–Calder Gap, which is the widest low-level gap in the Pennines and a route used since prehistoric times, Gargrave has road, canal and rail links within its boundaries. The Romans built a trans-Pennine road to the south of the town and, in more settled times, a prosperous local Roman family built their villa nearby. The A65 still follows the route of the Kendal to Keighley turnpike, which was opened in 1753 in order to bring Westmorland wool more easily to the mills of the West Riding. In 1770, an Act of Parliament authorised the building of a canal to link Leeds to the Atlantic seaport of Liverpool but it took over 20 years to complete this difficult piece of water navigation. The men who navigated or built the canals became known as 'navvies', a title which is still used to describe anyone who is engaged in heavy manual building work. The Leeds–Liverpool canal is the oldest of the three trans-Pennine canals and the only one still navigable. It is now used by holiday boats. With the coming of the railway era, canals began to lose their commercial traffic. The Leeds to Carlisle railway was opened in 1876; the line from Gargrave runs north to Settle and the start of the scenic Settle to Carlisle line.

Travellers of a uniquely modern variety pass through Gargrave today in a steady stream along the Pennine Way. Here it follows one of its lowest and more rural sections, a link between the heather moors above Earby and the limestone wonders of Malham Cove.

On this walk, the canal is followed all the way from Gargrave as far as East Marton, where the Pennine Way is joined. Lush green fields lining a series of low hummocky. hills are crossed by the well-marked path used by the Pennine Way on its journey from East Marton to Gargrave.

A Old wharfs and canal-side buildings have been adapted for modern use as grain warehouses and offices. Today, mostly pleasure craft use the canal but the very rare commercial boat still plys its leisurely way through a section of the countryside which has remained unchanged for over 200 years.

B Locks enable canal traffic to climb up and down hills. Wider sections of the canal serve the dual purpose of storing water needed to supply the locks and of providing 'winding holes' or turning places for the boats.

C Early canal builders preferred to use the contours of the land, thereby reducing the need for a large number of locks, which are expensive to build and maintain and also require a great deal of water to work them.

D The walk follows the well-signposted Pennine Way route from East Marton all the way to Gargrave.

E Viewpoint. Gargrave and the wild limestone moors of Upper Airedale can be glimpsed from Scaleber Hill. The green hummocky landscape is made from boulder clay deposited by retreating glaciers and melt waters after they had breached the Aire Gap during the last Ice Age. The rolling nature of the countryside is unsuitable for extensive ploughing but makes excellent grazing for dairy cattle.

Walk 15
SIMON'S SEAT

0 _____ 1 mile

0 _____ 1 km

4 miles (6.4 km) Strenuous; one climb of 1122 feet (342 m)

The best approach is by way of Appletreewick, which is off the B6160. Drive down the Barden Bridge road for ½ mile (0.8 km). Park beyond the bridge below Howgill chapel.

Appletreewick — the locals pronounce it 'Ap'trick' — has two pubs and both supply meals.

Several old houses, at least 400 years old, indicate the age of this village. It was once classed as a township, being granted a charter in 1311 to hold an annual Onion Fair.

Simon's Seat, the high point of this walk, is on Barden Fell grouse moor. Although access is

free for most of the year, there will be days when the moor is closed for shooting, or during drought and periods of high fire risk. Check locally with the Chatsworth Estate Office (01756 710533) or the Yorkshire Dales National Park Information Centre (01756 752748).

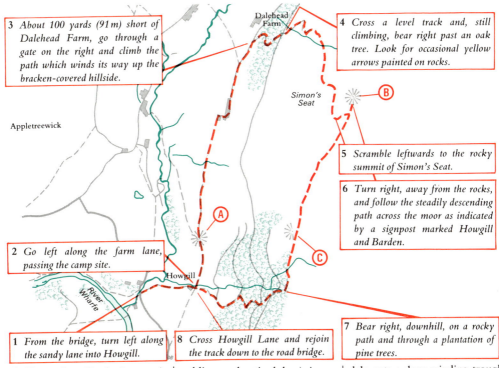

3 *About 100 yards (91 m) short of Dalehead Farm, go through a gate on the right and climb the path which winds its way up the bracken-covered hillside.*

4 *Cross a level track and, still climbing, bear right past an oak tree. Look for occasional yellow arrows painted on rocks.*

5 *Scramble leftwards to the rocky summit of Simon's Seat.*

6 *Turn right, away from the rocks, and follow the steadily descending path across the moor as indicated by a signpost marked Howgill and Barden.*

2 *Go left along the farm lane, passing the camp site.*

7 *Bear right, downhill, on a rocky path and through a plantation of pine trees.*

1 *From the bridge, turn left along the sandy lane into Howgill.*

8 *Cross Howgill Lane and rejoin the track down to the road bridge.*

Appletreewick

Dalehead Farm

Simon's Seat

Howgill

River Wharfe

A Viewpoint. Barden's woodlands cloak Lower Wharfedale with Barden Moor as their backcloth. Fir Beck joins the main dale directly below the viewpoint. Parcevall Hall, with its attractive gardens (open to the

public on advertised days), is upstream of Fir Beck and beyond the hall is Trollers Gill, a narrow ravine with an eerie echo.

B Viewpoint. The view makes the climb worthwhile. Wharfe-

dale cuts a deep winding trough to the north and the broad spread of Ilkley Moor is to the south.

C Viewpoint of the hamlet and farmsteads of Howgill sheltering below a tree-covered hillock.

0   1 mile

0   1 km

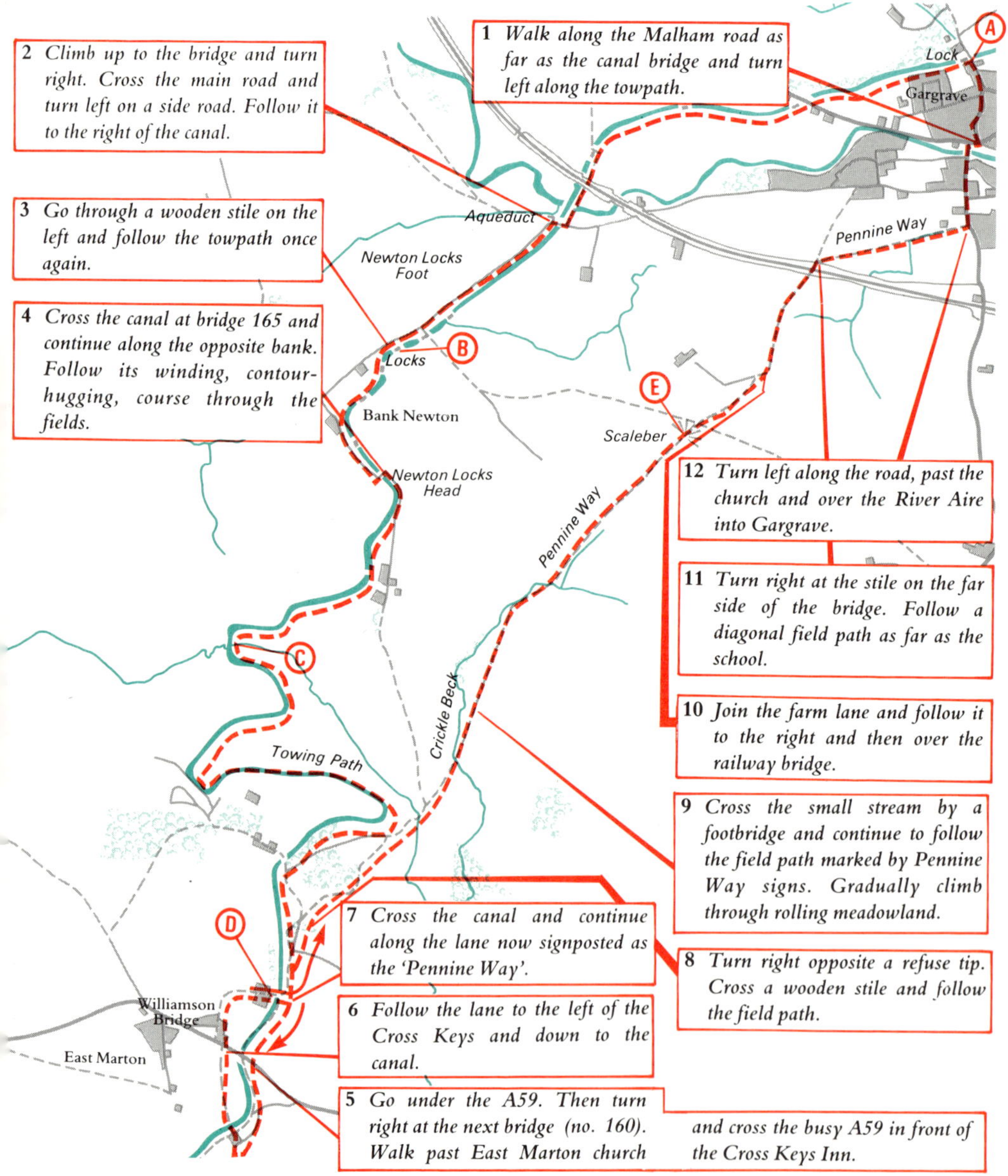

1 Walk along the Malham road as far as the canal bridge and turn left along the towpath.

2 Climb up to the bridge and turn right. Cross the main road and turn left on a side road. Follow it to the right of the canal.

3 Go through a wooden stile on the left and follow the towpath once again.

4 Cross the canal at bridge 165 and continue along the opposite bank. Follow its winding, contour-hugging, course through the fields.

5 Go under the A59. Then turn right at the next bridge (no. 160). Walk past East Marton church and cross the busy A59 in front of the Cross Keys Inn.

6 Follow the lane to the left of the Cross Keys and down to the canal.

7 Cross the canal and continue along the lane now signposted as the 'Pennine Way'.

8 Turn right opposite a refuse tip. Cross a wooden stile and follow the field path.

9 Cross the small stream by a footbridge and continue to follow the field path marked by Pennine Way signs. Gradually climb through rolling meadowland.

10 Join the farm lane and follow it to the right and then over the railway bridge.

11 Turn right at the stile on the far side of the bridge. Follow a diagonal field path as far as the school.

12 Turn left along the road, past the church and over the River Aire into Gargrave.

Map labels: Lock, Gargrave, Aqueduct, Pennine Way, Newton Locks Foot, Locks, Bank Newton, Scaleber, Newton Locks Head, Pennine Way, Crickle Beck, Towing Path, Williamson Bridge, East Marton

A B C D E

31